LITTLE BIGHORN BATTLEFIELD

HISTORIC LANDMARKS

Jason Cooper

The Rourke Book Company, Inc.
Vero Beach, Florida 32964

PHOTO CREDITS:
© Steve Warble: cover, title page, pages 4, 7, 8 12, 13, 17; © James P. Rowan: pages 10, 15, 18, 21

PRODUCED & DESIGNED by East Coast Studios
eastcoaststudios.com

EDITORIAL SERVICES:
Janice L. Smith for Penworthy Learning Systems

Library of Congress Cataloging-in-Publication Data

Cooper, Jason, 1942-
    Little Bighorn Battlefield / Jason Cooper.
        p. cm. — (Historic Landmarks)
    ISBN 1-55916-325-9
    1. Little Bighorn, Battle of the, Mont., 1876 v Juvenile literature. 2. Little Bighorn Battlefield National Monument (Mont.)—Juvenile literature. [1. Little Bighorn, Battle of the, Mont., 1876. 2. Little Bighorn Battlefield National Monument (Mont.) 3. National monuments.] I. Title.

E83.876 .C7 2000
973.8'2—dc21
                                        00–038727

TABLE OF CONTENTS

LITTLE BIGHORN BATTLEFIELD

Wild grasses still cover the hills and bend in **prairie** (PRAIR ee) winds. Cottonwood trees still stand in the green valley of the Little Bighorn River.

This is the Little Bighorn Battlefield National Monument. The land looks now much the same as it did then, on June 25, 1876. And now it's a safe place to visit. (Just stay clear of rattlesnakes, the National Park Service warns.)

A stone marker for one of General Custer's soldiers rests in a meadow of needlelike yucca plants and prairie grass.

On June 25, 1876, this open, rolling country was a killing field. It was a graveyard for men and their horses. Hundreds of men died in a battle here between Plains Indians and American soldiers, the "blue coats."

That battle is often remembered as "Custer's Last Stand" or "The Battle of the Little Bighorn." It was the last big battle of the Indian Wars on the plains.

Last Stand Monument recalls the more than 200 cavalrymen who died here on June 25, 1876.

BVT. MAJ. GEN'L G. A. CUSTER.
CAPTAINS.
M. W. KEOGH.
G. W. YATES.
T. W. CUSTER.
LIEUTENANTS.
W. W. COOKE.
A. E. SMITH.
DONALD McINTOSH.
JAMES CALHOUN.
J. E. PORTER.
B. H. HODGSON.
J. G. STURGIS.
W. VAN W. REILY.
J. J. CRITTENDEN.
H. M. HARRINGTON.
J. M. DE WOLF.
G. E. LORD.
SOLDIERS.
CHRISTOPHER CRIDDLE.
RICH'D FARRELL.
IN MEMORY OF
OFFICERS AND SOLDIERS WHO FELL NEAR THIS PLACE,
FIGHTING WITH THE 7TH UNITED STATES CAVALRY,
AGAINST SIOUX INDIANS,
ON THE 25TH AND 26TH OF JUNE,
A. D. 1876.

The Battle of the Little Bighorn is one of the most famous battles fought in America. Perhaps only the Alamo and the great Civil War Battle of Gettysburg are as well-known.

Here, on the hills above the Little Bighorn River, General George A. Custer and 263 of the men of his group, the Seventh **Cavalry** (KAV ul ree), were killed. They died at the hands of perhaps 1,500-2,000 Indian warriors. Most were Cheyenne, Sioux, and Arapaho. They fought under such war leaders as Crazy Horse, Gall, Crow King, Two Moons, and Left Hand.

A distant rainbow lights the sky behind the Little Bighorn Battlefield National Monument.

The Indians fought to defend their vanishing way of life and homeland. They fought not only with skill and courage. They fought with anger and bitterness. The whites, they felt, had too often lied to them about where and how they could live.

General Custer's cavalry unit had come west with other army units. Their job was to force the Indians onto **reservations** (rez er VAY shunz). Some Indians were already on reservations. Hundreds more, however, had refused to go. So the army's horse soldiers were sent out by the U.S. Government to remove these **hostile** (HAHS tul) Indians—one way or another.

Near the battlefield, the Little Bighorn River valley was the site of a huge Indian camp in June, 1876.

The national cemetery at the battlefield has been a military graveyard for soldiers from several wars. General Custer is buried at the U.S. Military Academy in West Point, New York.

After the Little Bighorn victory, Sitting Bull led many of the Indians to Canada, away from the reach of the U.S. Army.

Custer did not lack bravery. But on June 25, 1876, he may have lacked good sense. He divided his soldiers among himself, Major Marcus Reno, and Captain Frederick Benteen. Then Custer rode with his group into a huge Indian camp along the Little Bighorn River. Custer attacked the village, but he was soon overpowered by hundreds of warriors.

The great luck and skill that had helped Custer survive bloody Civil War (1861-1865) battles left him. As Little Bighorn Battlefield historian John Doerner says, "Custer was outnumbered, outgunned, and outfought."

Private Thomas Meador was killed on June 26, the second day of fighting for the Reno-Benteen command.

Everyone who rode with Custer himself died. Among them were the general's brothers, Tom and Boston. Custer's brother-in-law, James Calhoun, and nephew, 18-year-old Autie Reed, died along with 206 others in the Custer command. Reno, Benteen, and their men were about 5 miles (8 kilometers) away. They found a good defensive position and held out against the Indians for 2 days. Reno, Benteen, and about 350 of their soldiers survived.

The Visitor Center and national cemetery lie below the markers on Last Stand Hill.

VISITING THE BATTLEFIELD

The national monument covers 765 acres (310 hectares) in 2 sections. Both sections are surrounded by Crow Indian land. The site is about 65 miles (104 kilometers) southeast of Billings, Montana.

A 5-mile (8-kilometer) roadway connects the 2 parts of the battlefield. Markers along the route explain the events, at least so far as they are known.

Sage (left) and yucca grow on the rough, windswept ground. Here Major Reno and Captain Benteen found enough cover to hold off the Indians for two days.

Markers also show where the cavalrymen and a few of the Indians fell during the battle. This is the only battlefield in the world that marks the places where men fell.

At Last Stand Hill, a visitor can stand close to where the general himself died. He was found here with 41 of his men and 39 dead horses. The horses' bodies had been used as shields against the whizzing arrows and bullets. The other 169 men in Custer's group were killed elsewhere on the battlefield.

Many of the Indian warriors at the Little Bighorn had better rifles than the soldiers they fought. A 7th Cavalry trooper would have worn this uniform and likely have carried this type of rifle in 1876.

The Reno-Benteen battle site is 5 miles (8 kilometers) from Last Stand Hill.

In 1999 the National Park Service announced plans to build a large, walk-in Indian Memorial at the battlefield. The Park Service has also begun to mark places where Indian warriors fell. Indian families first marked those places with rock piles after the battle.

No one knows how many Indian warriors died. Modern studies of the battlefield, though, suggest that the number was under 100.

GLOSSARY

cavalry (KAV ul ree) — a unit of soldiers on horses

hostile (HAHS tul) — one who is your enemy; to act extremely unfriendly or angry toward

prairie (PRAIR ee) — the original grassland of much of western and midwestern North America

reservation (rez er VAY shun) — an area whose size was decided by the U.S. Government and on which Indians were sent to live

INDEX

FURTHER READING

Find out more about Little Bighorn Battlefield National Monument and Custer's Last Stand with these helpful books and information sites:

Krehbiel, Randy. *Little Bighorn.* Twenty-First Century, 1997.
Stein, Conrad R. *Battle of the Little Bighorn.* Childrens Press, 1997.

Little Bighorn Battlefield National Monument
   www.nps.gov/libi